THE BASIC GUIDE TO UNDERSTANDING OPTIONS AND TECHNICAL ANALYSIS

AND STRATEGIES FOR THEIR USE

By

Thomas H. Yarborough

ISBN: 1-4033-8285-9 (e-book)
ISBN: 1-4033-8286-7 (Paperback)
ISBN: 1-4033-8287-5 (RocketBook)

Library of Congress Control Number: 2002095134

This book is printed on acid free paper.

Printed in the United States of America
Bloomington, IN

1stBooks – rev. 01/29/03

THE HARDEST PART OF INVESTING IS

AVOIDING THE DOGS

INDEX

Chapter One   What Is An Option?........................ 1

Chapter Two   When You Are Bearish, Put On

                    The Option 12

Chapter Three   Selling Puts 18

Chapter Four   Combinations 30

Chapter Five   Writing Call Strategies 33

                    Repair Strategies 39

                    Buy Time In The Money, Sell

                    Premium Out Of The Money 46

                    Stop Orders 55

Chapter Six   61

                    Spreads.. 61

                    Bull Spread 61

                    Bear Spread..................................... 65

Calendar Spreads 70

Options And Retirement Accounts . 72

Short Stock Short Put...................... 73

Chapter Seven 77

Picking A Stock To Write Calls

Against 77

Insider Buying And Selling 84

Institutional Holdings...................... 86

Chapter Eight   Technical Analysis........................... 87

Chapter Nine 98

Shorter Term Indicators 98

Weekly And Monthly Moving

Averages 100

Bollinger Bands 103

Stochastics..................................... 106

On Balance Volume....................... 109

MACD 113

Support, Resistance And Trend

Lines 116

Point And Figure Charting............ 119

Accumulation/Distribution

Line 123

Common   Topping   And

Bottoming Chart Patterns 125

Double Top 125

Double Bottom............................. 127

Head And Shoulder....................... 129

Fibonacci Numbers....................... 132

VIX 135

Chapter Ten   140

The Wash Rule 140

Excerpts 145

Something Else To Consider… 156

Quiz... 161

Answer Page 171

OPTIONS, WHAT ARE THEY

GOOD FOR...

ABSOLUTELY EVERYTHING...

In the 32 years that I have spent as a stockbroker/financial advisor / financial consultant/investment advisor...or whatever the term de jour happened to be, I have seen a transition from the stockbroker who was a "stock jockey" to the investment advisor who is a "money manager asset gatherer". The transition has taken place, in my opinion, because of the lawsuits that materialized from individual brokers picking their own stocks (with or without the help of the brokerage house analyst recommendation).

The sad part about this transition is that the Wall Street brokerage houses clamped down on brokers doing any kind of creative strategies. Wall Street brokerage firms only wanted their brok...that is to say, their investment advisors to raise assets and put their clients' money with money managers and collect the wrap fees.

The good news about this strategy is that the incentive for "stockbrokers" to "churn" client's accounts is now taken away by the introduction of wrap fee business. The bad news is that, from what I have witnessed, the investment advisors have less of a "hands on" approach to the client once their money is invested with a money manager.

There were those clients who wished to trade their own stocks in a wrap account, but the firms put a limit on the amount of transactions that could take place in a wrap account. Because there was less incentive for a broker to give investment ideas to the client, it was my experience that asset gatherers did little to educate the client on writing calls against stock positions.

The saddest thing that took place in this transition of stock jockey to asset gatherer is that the asset gatherer knew little of the "nuts and bolts" of the craft as the stock jockey once did.

In 2001 I did $985,000 in commissions as a foreign institutional broker, all at a nickel a share commission. That means that I traded 19,700,000 shares of stock and option contracts.

I enjoyed the fact that many of the traders at these foreign institutions would ask my advice about which options to write against which stocks. And since I enjoyed technical analysis, they would often ask me where support and resistance were on various indices and stocks.

But there were over 30 brokers in that office and only 2 or 3 of them did any option business at all. And why was that? Lawsuits.

The term "options" strikes fear in the hearts of many people because it is considered to be highly speculative. It is considered to be so highly speculative that at many Wall Street firms one is not even allowed to open an option account if one is past the age of 70. This means that with money market rates currently at 1%, an individual who wishes to get more income than that by buying General Electric stock and writing calls against it is not allowed to do so. I think that is sad. It is especially sad when you take into consideration the amount of corporate "accounting creativity" that has taken place.

It is for this reason that I am writing this book in hopes that someone somewhere will read it and make a little bit of money from its contents.

CHAPTER ONE

What is an option?

In the early 1980's, Miami Beach put it to the voters as to whether to allow gambling or not. If gambling was allowed, the real estate value in Miami Beach would double overnight. So how was a person to benefit? Should a hotel tycoon buy up one of the hotels in hopes that the voters passed gambling? The real estate values had already started to creep up in hopes that gambling would pass.

But what if it didn't pass? The buyer of the hotel would have to turn around and sell it and probably take a huge loss.

What about an option?

1

Well, that is exactly what one tycoon did. He went to one hotel owner and told him that he would give him 5% of the present value of his hotel for the right to buy the hotel at a 25% premium in 30 days. So the hotel was worth (hypothetically) $10,000,000 and the hotel owner gets $500,000 for the right to have the hotel bought from him at $12,500,000 within 30 days? Why wouldn't he take it?

And so gambling didn't pass. The hotel owner was $500,000 richer and still had his hotel. The tycoon was happy because he didn't have a hotel he had to unload (and pay a 3% brokerage fee on both sides of the transaction). That's not to say he wouldn't have been much happier if gambling had gone through.

So there is a very simple explanation of an option transaction. The buyer is the speculator that is controlling a $10,000,000 asset for $500,000. The seller is the conservative individual who owns the asset and is looking for the cash flow from the sale of the option. In this case he made 5% on his money in 30 days. If he could do that every 30 days he would make 60% on his money a year.

So translate this into stock terms. Mr. Smith owns 100 shares of Microsoft Corp which he paid $50 a share for and the stock is now $50 a share. Mr. Jones tells Mr. Smith that he will give him $250.00 for the right to buy his stock from him at $50 per share within the next 30 days. Each call option is on 100 shares of stock. You can not buy or sell calls against fractional shares (in the case of

Thomas H. Yarborough

stock splits there are fractional shares attached to each call but as a general rule each call or put option is on 100 share lots).

Mr. Smith will be making 5% on his money if the stock stays below $50 a share for the next 30 days ($250 divided by $5000).

So why would Mr. Jones want to blow his money like this? Well, why do so many people go to Las Vegas every year? It's true that Wall Street doesn't give you free booze and cigarettes while you are buying options (although if things don't get better on Wall Street pretty soon they may resort to that or giving away toasters with every 100 options purchased), buying call or put options is gambling most of the time. The payoff can be pretty high when a home run is hit however.

*For simplicity sake, all calculations will not include transaction costs which must be considered. For those trading through a discount broker online (or have a fee based account) the transaction cost will make a minuscule difference in the results.

Let's take the case of Mr. Smith and Mr. Jones again. Let's say that Microsoft reports earnings that are 20% greater than the Wall Street analysts are looking for and Microsoft jumps up to $70 by option expiration date. Mr. Jones paid Mr. Smith $250 for the right to take the stock away from him at $50 a share. So his $250 is now worth $2000 ($70 per share times 100 shares is $7000 minus $5000 <100 shares at $50> = $2000). Mr. Smith made 5% on his money in one month but Mr. Jones made $800% on his money in one month.

But what if Mr. Jones doesn't have the $5000 to pay Mr. Smith for his 100 shares of Microsoft at

$50? Well, in reality options trade on an exchange. Just as Microsoft trades on the NASDAQ, and General Electric trades on the New York Stock Exchange, so do Microsoft call and put options trade on the CBOE (Chicago Board Option Exchange) or the American Stock Exchange or the Philadelphia Stock Exchange or the Pacific Stock Exchange.

So on option expiration day, with Microsoft trading at $70 per share, the Microsoft call for that month will be trading at $20.00 per call. It will be trading at "intrinsic value". In other words all of the "time premium" will have evaporated in the option because there is no time left in the option.

A week before option expiration the Microsoft $50 call might have been trading at $19.00 with

Microsoft stock trading at $68.00. That would have meant that the call had a one point "time premium" left in it (the time premium is the actual price of the option...in this case $19.00...minus the intrinsic value of the option...in this case $18.00 <since the call is a $50 call and the stock is at $68 then the option is 18 points "in the money">).

So in this case, Mr. Smith is the casino and Mr. Jones is the player. Unfortunately for Mr. Jones, the cards are stacked against him since he is playing with a depreciating asset. Each day that goes by the time premium ticks away. I read 20 years ago that 90% of all options expire worthless. What casino in the world would not want those odds?

To determine the time premium in an option you must first figure the intrinsic value of the option and then subtract it from the actual price of the option. For example, if IBM is selling at $67 a share and the $65 call is selling at $4 what is the time premium? First, you must find the intrinsic value. With IBM selling at $67 it has a REAL value of $2 a share since the option is to CALL the stock at $65 a share. If the option is selling at $4 and the intrinsic value is only $2 then the time premium is anything above that $2. So the time premium is also $2 ($4 - $2 = $2).

Getting back to the Microsoft option, when you think about it, there are four things that the underlying stock (in this case Microsoft) can do.

1) The stock can go down...in which case Mr. Jones loses all his money.

2) The stock can stay at $50…in which case Mr. Jones loses all his money.

3) The stock can go up, but less than the 2 ½ points that Mr. Jones invested in the option (remember he paid $250 for the call option which is translates into a 2 ½ point move in Microsoft). In this case Mr. Jones loses only a portion of his money. If Microsoft is at $51 on option expiration day then the option will have an intrinsic value of $1 or $100 for 100 shares of stock. Since Mr. Jones invested $250 (plus commissions) he will be out $150 (less commissions on the sale of the option).

4) The stock can go up more than the 2 ½ points needed for Mr. Jones to break even.

This is the only example of the four in which Mr. Jones will make any money.

When you consider that 90% of all options expire worthless and one only has a one in four probability in the movement of the underlying stock of making money, it seems that the "house" has an undue advantage.

The thing that gets many people confused is the terminology CALL and PUT. The way that I was taught 32 years ago helped me tremendously and it is extremely simple.

When you want to make a telephone CALL you pick UP the phone. When you are through talking you PUT DOWN the phone. So if you think a stock is going to go UP then you buy a CALL. If you think a stock is going to go DOWN then you buy a

PUT.

CHAPTER TWO

WHEN YOU ARE BEARISH PUT ON

THE OPTION

So we are in a "Bear" market and your next door neighbor has been making a killing in the market by shorting 1000 shares of Yahoo at $240 a share and now it is down to $10. He has made $230,000 but now he is covering his short position, locking in his profit and he has a new stock, ABC Corp that he thinks is an excellent short and it is selling at $80 a share. He tells you about the stock and he thinks that the stock is going to $5 a share.

You are too embarrassed to tell him that you don't have the necessary funds to short this stock. Or perhaps you are just plain afraid to short a stock. Shorting stocks is highly speculative and the risk is unlimited. Remember when you buy a stock at $80 a share, the most you can lose is $80 a share. When you short a stock at $80 a share however, your risk is unlimited. What if Warren Buffet decides that he likes the company and decides to buy them out for $180 a share?

The put option enables you to participate on the downside without risking $80 per share. Let's assume that the option premium on the put is 5% as was the case in our last example using Microsoft calls. A 5% premium on an $80 stock would mean that the $80 put would be selling for $4 or $400 would be the cost to own one put in ABC Corp at $80 for 30 days.

So let's assume that ABC Corp does go down as your neighbor predicted and the stock falls to $60 in the 30 day before your option expires. In this case your $400 speculation is now worth $2000 ($80 - $60 = 20 x 100 shares = $2000).

But what if your neighbor is wrong and what if Warren Buffet were to make a tender offer for the stock at $180 a share. Let's say that your neighbor only shorted 100 shares of stock at $80 but now the stock is $180. He lost $10,000 ($180 - $80 = $100 x 100 shares = $10,000). But you have only lost the $400 that you paid for the put option.

Put options are not just used to speculate that a stock or stock index is going to go down. You can use a put option as an insurance policy.

Let's say that you own 1000 shares of General Electric that you inherited from your father and the cost basis is $10 a share. General Electric is now selling at $40 a share and you don't want to sell the stock for sentimental reasons and you also are not very keen on the idea of paying capital gains on $20,000 if you sell the stock. You could buy 10 puts on General Electric.

In the prior examples of Microsoft and ABC Corporation I used examples of options that would expire in 30 days. You can also buy or sell options going out as far as 2 or 3 years (they are called "leaps" when they go out a year or more). So in the case of General Electric you may pay a 20-25% premium for a $40 put option going out one year.

In that case you would be paying $8000 to $10,000 for that insurance policy.

But what if you don't have the $8000 to $10,000 to pay for the puts? Well, in that case you can always sell "out of the money" calls and buy "out of the money puts.

For example: if General Electric is selling at $40 a share, it is likely that the leap $45 call and the leap $35 put will be selling for close to the same price. So if you sold the $45 leap calls, you could use the proceeds to buy the $35 leap puts. Let's assume that, in this case, they are both selling for $2 per option. The $45 leap call is selling for $2 per call and the $35 leap put is selling for $2 per put.

You would sell 10 of the $45 leap calls @ $2 and bring in $2000 less commissions (each call is $200 x

10 = $2000) and you would buy 10 of the $35 leap puts @ $2 and pay $2000 plus commissions.

Now let's flash forward one year and assume that you were right about your fears and the stock is now selling at $15 per share. You now have two choices.

1) You can "exercise" your put and "put" the stock to the person who sold you the leap put at $35 per share and collect $35000.

2) You can sell the 10 puts at $20 ($2000 per put) and bring in $20,000 and hold onto the stock.

In either case you are going to have a capital gains problem but in both cases it will be long term capital gains (make sure the leap puts expire past the time that is necessary for it to be long term).

CHAPTER THREE

SELLING PUTS

Sometimes an option premium can be so attractive and the underlying stock can be considered so attractive, that you can't understand why anyone would buy a put at those ridiculous prices.

Let's say that you like Microsoft stock, and it is selling for $40 a share after selling off from $80 a share. You look at the $30 leap put going out two years and you see it is selling for $3.00. That means that if you sell that put naked, the person would be putting the stock to you at $30.00 per share. And with the additional $3 you bring in from selling the put naked, you will actually own the stock at $27 if

it is put to you at $30 (30 − 3 put premium = $27)
Since you don't believe Microsoft will ever get to
$30, you sell the put naked.*

You can then do one of two things:

1) Stay naked the put until option expiration in
   two years. (Since you get the premium right
   away you can spend it on what you want as
   long as you maintain the margin
   requirements on a naked put position in the
   margin account).

2) If the stock rallies (hence the underlying put
   option would decrease in value) you could
   buy the put option back for a profit.

---

* means uncovered or not owning the underlying security.

Not everyone can be approved for naked put option writing. The net worth requirements vary from firm to firm and can range from a $100,000 net worth to a $500,000 net worth depending on the firm. And if you are over 70 years of age you can forget it in most cases.

I did meet an interesting gentleman, I will call him Mr. M., who did happen to be well past age 70 and who also managed to have an account at Merrill Lynch where he was doing "naked put spreads" in blue chip stocks. The man had been referred to me by an ex-employer of mine. We had parted amicably and when Mr. M. came to his office looking for someone who specialized in equity option strategies, my friend referred him to me.

Mr. M. had an account in excess of $40,000,0000.00 which consisted mostly of laddered (putting a portion of the money in different maturities, so that he has some bonds maturing each year) U.S. Treasury notes. What he would do is to short "out-of-the-money" puts in a blue chip stock that he liked, let's say General Electric, and he would then buy still further out of the money puts for protection. The credit difference in the spread would be kept by Mr. M.

For an example, I took a current quote from General Electric. General Electric closed last night at $30.15 while the October 30 put which expires in 6 weeks is selling at $1.80 and the October 27 ½ put is selling at $1.00.

Mr. M. would sell the General Electric October 30 put at 1.80 and buy the October 27 ½ put at $1.00. His account would be credited with $0.80 per option. That may not seem like much money, but if you do the math, it works out to be a considerable amount of money.

Mr. M. would use the collateral of the Treasury notes (there was a 90% release or borrowing power on the notes) to use toward his margin requirement on the naked put spreads. The margin requirement for naked puts is roughly 20-30% of the underlying stock value (it depends on the firm as to what the requirements are). So if, for example, one were to short 1000 puts (equivalent to 100,000 shares of stock) in General Electric "at the money" October

30's, the requirements would be 20 or 30% of $3,000,000 or $600,000 to $900,000.

Since Mr. M. had $40,000,000 in Treasury Notes that had a borrowing power of 90% of that, his borrowing power was $38,000,000. So a $600,000 or $900,000 margin requirement on 1000 puts would use up less than 3% of the loan value. Mr. M. would bring in $80,000 (less commissions) from the proceeds of these naked spreads ($0.80 or $80.00 per put contract times 1000 puts). He would then put the $80,000 into the money market for the six week period and earn the money market rate on the money for that period of time until the October options expired.

On option expiration day, Mr. M. had to make a decision if the stock was below $30 a share. He had to decide whether to close out the position (buy back his short 30 put and sell out the 27 ½ put) or to allow them to put the stock to him.

Basically three things could occur on option expiration:

1) General Electric could be trading above $30 a share, in which case both the short (30) puts expire worthless and the long (27 ½) puts expire worthless. This is a best case scenario as Mr. M. makes his $80,000 and is free to do it again.

2) General Electric is trading below $30 a share but above $27 ½ a share. In this case the $27 ½ puts that he was long (owned) would expire and he would lose the money that he paid for those puts (he paid $1.00 per put or $100 times 1000

puts = $100,000). He would also have to buy back the $30 put. Let's assume that General Electric closed at $28 on option expiration day. In this case he would lose all of his money ($100,000) in the 27 ½ puts that he was long (owned) and he would have to buy back the $30 puts, since they are 2 points in the money. At intrinsic value the puts should be selling for $2.00 or $200 per put ($30 - $28 = $2) x 1000 puts. His cost for buying back his short October 30 puts would be $200,000. So his cost for closing out the entire position was $300,000 ($100,000 for the October 27 ½ puts which expired worthless and $200,000 for the October 30 puts). Since he only brought in $80,000 (plus $184 interest he earned from the money market for six weeks), his total loss on the transaction is $220,000 ($300,000 minus $80,000). Of course, Mr. M. can always do nothing and allow the person to "put" the stock to him at $30. He can then write calls against that position once he is long the stock.

3) The other possibility is that General Electric falls below 27 ½. Let's assume in this case that there is tremendously bad news on General Electric and the stock has fallen to $20.00 per share on option expiration. In this case Mr. M. can do one of two things. He can either "close out" both sides of the "spread" (buy back the short October 30 put and sell out the long 27 ½ put) which will cost him $250,000 ($30 - $ 27.50 = $250 times 1000= $250,000). His loss in this case is $250,000 minus

the $80,000 that he brought in originally or $170,000. He can also elect to have the stock put to him at $30.00 a share and immediately exercise his $27.50 puts. The cost would still be $250,000 but the transaction costs may be much less for exercising (same as buying or selling the stock) then it might be for buying and selling the puts. For example, the cost of buying and selling options at some on line brokerage firms is $1.00 to $1.50 per option which in this case would amount to $2000 to $3000. (1000 $27.50 puts and 1000 $30 puts) whereas buying and selling the shares (exercising the $27 ½ puts and allowing the stock to be put to him) may result in a transaction fee of $9.00 or $16.00 depending on what the on line firm charges for market order transactions.

With this strategy, Mr. M. knows that the most that he can lose in any given case is 2 ½ points minus what he brought in (in this case .80). So Mr. M. knew that no matter what happened with General Electric during that six week period that he was short the spread, the most he could gain was $0.80 and the most he could lose was $1.70 ($2.50 - $0.80). This is a form of risk management.

Of course the opposite side of this strategy can be taken as well. In an earlier chapter we had discussed buying a put on ABC Corp at $80 because we were of the belief that the stock would go down. If we had sold the $80 CALL and bought the $82.50 CALL(assuming that there was an $82.50 CALL) and applied the same spread (.80) to it, the results would have been less impressive than buying the

puts. We had made $16,000 ($20,000 less our cost

of $4000) by going long the $80 puts on ABC Corp.

Buy if we had instead done this $80-$82 ½ spread

for $0.80, we would have only made $800 on 10

spreads. Our risk would have been $1700 ($250-

$80 x 10) whereas our risk in owning the puts was

$4000 (the cost of the puts).

CHAPTER FOUR

COMBINATIONS

There are times when it might be a good idea to buy a combination of a put and a call. Let's say that Microsoft is selling at $50.00 a share and is sitting on support*. Earnings are due out for Microsoft, and if the earnings are good, then support* will hold and the stock could bounce up to its resistance ** level at $60.00. But if the support* at $50 breaks, the next support level is at $40.00. What should you do?

Let's assume again that the premium on the $50 call and put option is 5% so that if Microsoft is selling at $50.00 the $50 call will be selling for $250.00 per call and the $50.00 put will be selling at

$250.00. So you buy one $50 put and one $50 call. Your total cost is $500 ($250 + $250).

Now let's assume that Microsoft misses the street estimate on their earnings and the stock falls to its next support* level at $40. The call will be worth little, if nothing, but the put will have an intrinsic value of $10 or $1000 ($50 strike price and the stock is selling at $40). So in this case you made 100% on your money if you sell the put (you can then either sell the call or elect to hope to "get lucky" and get a bounce in the stock at which time you can maybe sell the call for a little more...but remember you are dealing with a depreciating asset).-

Let's assume now that Microsoft beat the street's earnings estimates and Microsoft runs up to

$60 a share. In that case the put side would be worthless and the call side would be worth $10 or $1000. Again you made 100%.

The risk here is obvious. As I stated in an earlier chapter, buying options is more speculative than selling covered options (owning the underlying stock). Because the depreciation in the option is going against you since you are the owner and not with you when you are the seller.

* support and resistance are technical terms which I will discuss in a later chapter

CHAPTER FIVE

WRITING CALL STRATEGIES

There are several factors that affect the premium that one will get in an option:

1) Time. The more time that is left in the option, the more "time premium" and hence the more expensive the option will be. For example, the September call has more premium than the August call and the October call will have more premium than the September call.

2) Closeness to the strike price. The closer the option is to the strike price the more premium will be in the option. For example if a stock is selling at $20, the $20 call will

cost more than the 22 ½ call and the 22 ½ call will cost more than the 25 call. However, the premium may actually be more in the 25 call than the 22 ½ call and the premium may actually be more than the 20 call. We will discuss this later.

3) Beta. The beta of the underlying stock is the volatility of the stock. The higher the beta, the more volatile the stock. If a stock has a beta of one, then this means that the stock is equal in volatility to the S+P 500. If a beta has beta of 2.0 it means that it is twice as volatile as the S+P 500. The greater the volatility of the stock the greater the premium should be. The buyer of the option will be speculating in the movement of the

underlying stock. If a stock is twice as volatile as the S+P 500 then there is twice the likelihood that his option will move as opposed to just sitting and depreciating until expiration. Say for example the S+P 500 has been trading in a 10% trading range, then a stock with a beta of 2.0 will statistically have a 20% trading range and a stock with a beta of 0.5 will have a 5% trading range. If you were a speculator and wished to buy an option on a stock, would you rather own an option on a stock with a beta of 0.5 or 2.0? The obvious answer is 2.0. Therefore the premium on the more volatile stock will be higher. This is a positive for someone who is looking to do covered calls however as it means that you will be bringing in a higher return on your option writing.

4) Interest rates. This is something that people tend to forget. The higher interest rates are, the higher the relative premiums will be in the options. The lower interest rates are the less the relative premiums will be in the options. Part of the logic for this is competitiveness of the marketplace. If a person can get 10% a year from an AAA government guaranteed bond (the last time that occurred was in the early 1980's) why would they be interested in getting 10% a year return from buying a common stock and selling the calls. The risk is much greater in the common stock than it is in the

AAA government guaranteed bonds. I exaggerated on this example, because even with interest rates currently (as of this writing) at 1% in money market rates, one can still get up to 10% a MONTH premiums in written calls. I will discuss this in a later chapter.

So if we look at the previous examples, it becomes clear that if one wishes to use option writing as a vehicle to generate income, one would be looking for a high beta stock in a high interest rate environment. (when I say high interest rates, I mean high REAL rates of return. If inflation is at 9% and interest rates are at 10% then the real rate after inflation is only 1%).

TIME: If one is looking to write calls, there are two approaches one can take regarding the amount of time to write the underlying call. It is my belief that as a general rule one should write the closest month when writing calls. This is not a rule written in stone and one must be flexible with this and look at each situation on a case by case basis.

In the present environment, interest rates are low and we have been in a bear market for three years (as of this writing). One of my favorite stocks has been Juniper Networks to write calls against. I have had much success in buying Juniper Networks under $7.50 a share and writing the nearest month 7.50 call against the stock. In the past year I have had the opportunity to do this on four separate occasions and three of those four times I was able to get .75 or better which amounted to a 10% return for that month. On one occasion I was unlucky enough to have the stock drop to $5 when the option expired and so I was only able to get $0.20 for the next month call (hind sight being 20-20 if I had waited for a bounce in the stock I could have gotten much more as the stock rallied up to $7 again in the next couple of weeks, but my strategy is to not wait.) Even getting $.20 for the call for one month resulted in a 3% return for that month. If you annualize that it is 36% a year.

REPAIR STRATEGIES

In this bear market there have been times that I have owned a stock and had it break support and fall precipitously from that point. In that case I must go out further than I would wish in time in order to bring in a realistic premium. A case in point is Nvidia Corporation.

As an institutional broker, I was working with a very bright young man, Benedikt, who was a trader at an Icelandic bank. We became good friends, and he always reminded me in looks as well as intelligence of Bill Gates. He was a strong believer in Nvidia Corporation and their product. And when the stock dropped down to 15 (from a high of 70) where there was substantial support, I looked at the near month calls options and they were selling for 2.25 or a 15% premium. My fear was that if the stock broke the support level of $15, the next support level was between $9 and $10 a share.

Although I usually try to find stocks that have a high premium but are selling below $10 to limit my downside, I could not resist the 15% premium in the option for one month despite my bearish tendency toward the overall market (especially technology).

Nvidia broke support and immediately dropped to just under $9 a share by option expiration. So despite the fact that I had made 15% on my money in one month, I now had to find an option to write with the stock at $9.00. When I looked at the next month $15 calls, they were selling at .20 bid. This amounted to only a 1 ½% return in one month. Now there are times when I will take 1 ½ % premium in one month when I have hope that the stock may rebound by expiration and the following month I will be able to get a much higher premium when the current month option expires.

I did not feel that confident when I looked at the chart on Nvidia however. I saw long term support at $5 and my general state of mind was pessimistic toward the market. So I waited for Nvidia to bounce off support. I then looked out to the March 15 calls which were selling at $2.00. This amounted to a 13% return for 7 months and would lower my cost basis down to below $11 in March if the stock was not called away (I paid $15 originally for the stock and brought in $2.25 from my first call write which lowered the cost basis to $12.75 {15-2.25=12.75} and by bringing in another $2.00 for the March calls it would lower my cost basis to

$10.75 (12.75-2.00=10.75). So that is what I begrudgingly did. This was my repair strategy.

The reason I do not like to write options that are far out in time is simple. Juniper is currently selling at $7.30 and the call which expires in six weeks is selling at .80. The call that expires in 4 months is selling at $1.50. I can either make 15% in one month (if the stock is taken away at 7.50) or I can make 29% on my money if the stock is taken away at 7.50 in 4 months.

You could look at the 15% in one month and say "that's easy if he makes 15% in one month then the call going out 4 months should be giving him 60%." That is a partial reason, but there is no guarantee that I can get 15% every month. This is a judgment call. I just don't wish to tie up money

Thomas H. Yarborough

for 4 months. If Juniper Networks exploded and ran up to $15.00 my investment in the stock would be locked up for 4 months and although 29% in four months is a very attractive return in this interest rate environment, I am of the impression that I can do better.

Some of you may be asking…"wait a minute, how did he come up with a 15% return? I only figured a 13.6% return." Well, if you divide 1.00 (.80 premium plus .20 capital gains…if it's called away at 7.50 there will be a .20 capital gain) by 7.30 it does come out to 13.6%, but one must remember that if you buy a stock and sell the call the same day, the proceeds from the sale of the call go TOWARD the purchase price. So in this case if you bought 1000 shares of Juniper Networks at 7.30 and you sold 10 thirty day 7.50 calls for .80, the amount that you would have to come up with would be $7300 (plus commissions) minus $800 (less commissions) or $6500 would be your out of pocket expense for the 1000 shares of Juniper Networks. And if the stock is called away at $7.50 then you will make $1000 on a $6500 investment or 15.3%.

It is hard to believe, but three years ago it was very simple to get 20% a month premium in calls. The downside was that these were in stocks that were wrapped up in the bubble, so that if you had been buying Juniper Networks at that time at $240 a share, you could have gotten $48.00 for a one month call, but what good would it have done you if the stock was sitting at $100 on option expiration day? This is another reason that I like to do the options on a month to month basis. If something disastrous happens with the stock you can always get out. Of course you can always get out of a position. All you need to do is buy back the call when you sell the stock.

BUY TIME IN THE MONEY, SELL PREMIUM OUT OF THE MONEY

When you are going to buy a put or call option is it best to allow yourself as much time as possible. The underlying stock should be chosen based on the merits of the stock, whether you are using fundamental or technical analysis. If the fundamentals or technical picture changes then you should exit the position. It does not matter whether you are long (or short) the stock or long (or short) the option, when the picture changes, exit.

Always determine the time "premium" that you are buying or selling. For example: If you like General Electric stock at $40 but you don't have the money to buy 100 shares of stock for $4,000 but you do have $800, you have several options (no pun intended). The nearest month has four call options. The General Electric 35 call options are selling at 5 ½; the nearest month 40 call is selling at 2 ½; the nearest month 45 call is selling at 1; and the nearest month 50 call is selling at ½.

You could buy only one 35 call for 5 ½ since you only have $800, or you could buy three 40 calls at 2 ½; or eight of the 45 calls at 1 (we assume no transaction costs here...as in a wrap account), and your last choice is you could buy 16 of the 50 calls at ½.

When making this decision, I prefer to look at the odds. Since one does not have a crystal ball that will tell them where the stock will be on option expiration day, you must calculate what the odds are of the option expiring worthless. Let us assume that there are 15 trading days left in this option. What are the odds of General Electric, which is currently selling at $40, being at $50 in 15 trading days? Pretty slim in the current bear market environment, so therefore, buying the 50 calls would not be my first choice. Looking at it from that perspective, the 35 calls are the safest way to go. The reward is not as great, but the risk is less.

The intrinsic value of the 35 call is 5 and the call is selling for 5 ½, therefore you are only paying a ½ point premium for 15 trading days. However, the premium on the 50 call is 10 ½ points. You are 10 points out of the money, which must be taken into consideration when determining time premium. So you add the amount you are out of the money plus the price you are paying for the option.

The greater the risk, the greater the reward most of the time and this time is no different. If you buy the 50 calls and the stock does not move 10 ½ points higher in the next 15 trading days, then you will have lost all of your money. However, let us assume that you buy 16 of the General Electric 50 calls at ½ and the stock shoots up to $55. In this case your $800 would now be worth $8000. You would make 1000% on your money.

If you only bought one call of the General Electric 35 calls at 5 ½, and the stock moved to $55, your $550 investment would be worth $2000 or you would have made 364% on your money. The percentages will increase the further out of the money you buy the calls because the risk is greater.

It is a judgment call as to which option to buy. If I write that one must ALWAYS buy the in the money calls to play it conservative, I am sure there is someone out there who will say that they always buy out of the money calls and make money. If they do then they are beating the odds by a huge amount. As I said earlier, 90% of all options expire worthless. By purchasing options that are out of the money you are increasing the odds that your options will expire worthless.

Getting back to the General Electric calls and your $800, we only looked at the near month calls. When you look at the calls going out 6 months you see that the quotes are as follows: The 35 calls are 6 ½, the 40 calls are 3 ½, the 45 calls are 2, and the 50 calls are 1 ¼.

In this case I would much rather pay 6 ½ for the General Electric calls going out six months, paying a 1 ½ point time premium than I would to pay a ½ point time premium for a call that expired in 15 trading days. There will be those who would say that they would rather buy the 50 calls for 1 ¼ going out six months and be able to control 600 shares of General Electric for the $800 rather than

100 shares by buying one of the 35 calls. This again is a judgment call. When it comes to buying calls I like to play it as conservatively as possible. I know that sounds like an oxymoron, because the term conservative should never be used when talking about going long calls.

When going long calls I like to buy in the money calls and give myself as much time as possible. In other words I like to pay as little premium as possible for the most amount of time.

When selling a covered call, the opposite is true most of the time. I like to sell the closest month and get as much premium as I can. When I say get the most premium, that does not mean that I wish to sell the in the money call to bring in the most money, that means that I wish to get the highest percentage return as possible, so I will most likely be selling the out of the money or "at" the money calls.

Assume that you bought 100 shares of General Electric and wish to sell one of the options mentioned in the previous paragraphs. In this case would you rather sell the General Electric 35 call for 5 ½ to make 1.5 % in 15 trading days (40 – 5 ½ = 34.5 divided into the time premium which is .5) or would you rather sell the near month 40 call for 2 ½ for a return of 6.7% in fifteen trading days? You could also sell the 45 call for 1 for a 2 ½ % return in 15 trading days.

Here again, if one knew where the stock was going to be in 15 trading days it would make the job much easier to determine which option to write. If the stock was going to be at $46, then you would much rather sell the $45 call for 1. If the stock is called away at $45 you would make 5 points gain on the stock plus the 1 point you got when you sold the call for a total of 6. Since you paid 39 for the stock (you paid 40 but you sold the option for 1 so 40 − 1 = 39), you made 15% on your money in 15 trading days.

On the other hand, if the stock is going to drop to 35 by option expiration day, you would much rather have written the 35 calls for 5 ½. You would only make 1 ½ %, but you would not have lost any money on paper on the stock (since you bought the stock at 40 and sold the calls at 5 ½, your out of pocket cost is 40 − 5 ½ = 34 ½).

So whether you are buying a call or selling a covered call, the bottom line is that it all depends on where the stock is going to be on option expiration day as to what your best option choice is going to be. I prefer to play the best odds.

STOP ORDERS

I mentioned before that if a stock goes against you to "stop yourself out". What I mean by this is to place a stop loss order with your broker or at least have a "mental" stop in mind to limit your losses.

I like to use technical analysis to determine my "stop loss" point. I may decide that if the 10 day moving average moves below the 50 day moving average that I will exit a position. Since I do not know at what price the stock will be if this occurs, I must keep an eye on the chart and enter the order the day this crossover occurs.

I may also see a stock in a sideways charting pattern where it will either break out to the upside if it gets above 50 or break down off the point and figure charts if it touches 45, so I will use a stop of 45. In this case I can tell my broker to enter a "Good until cancelled" order to sell 100 shares of XYZ at 45 stop.

This means that if XYZ trades at or below 45, my order immediately becomes a "market" order. There may be, however, other stop orders in ahead of me, so I may not be the next "tick" (trade) after the stock trades at 45.

The problem with putting this order in "Good until cancelled" (the order will be in every day until it is either filled or cancelled) is that the stock may "gap" down one morning below 45 and you will be filled around the price that it opens.

Let us assume that XYZ closed at $46 and you have an order in to sell 100 XYZ at 45 on a stop GTC (Good until cancelled). The next morning XYZ reports bad earnings and the stock opens for trading at $30 and immediately trades down to $29 ½. Your order that is in at 45 stop will be filled somewhere between $30 and $29 ½. Your "stop" will be triggered at $30 and you will then be put in at the market and get filled.

There are two ways to avoid this. The first is to just put the stop loss order in each day the other way is to put a "stop limit" order in.

Thomas H. Yarborough

A "stop limit" order would be put in as: sell 100 XYZ at 45 stop on a 45 limit Good until cancelled. This means that if the stock touches 45 your order automatically becomes a LIMIT order at 45 not a market order, so if the stock opens at $30 your order will not be executed.

This is a dual edge sword because the stock can trade at 45 and the next trade can be 44 7/8, 44 ¾, etc. and you will not be executed on your stop limit order. If you look in the paper the next day and see that the stock closed at 41 you may kick yourself for not putting a straight stop loss order in.

GOOD UNTIL CANCELLED ORDERS

One more word on Good Until Cancelled orders. If you put in a good until cancelled order to buy 100 shares of XYZ at 40 you must be cognizant as to whether there is a dividend on XYZ or not. If a stock goes "ex-dividend" then all good until cancelled buy orders are adjusted in price.

Let us assume that XYZ pays a $2.00 a year dividend. Every quarter it will pay a $.50 dividend and so every quarter the stock will trade "ex-dividend" $.50 on a given day.

Going "ex-dividend" simply means that they adjust the opening price of the stock down by 50 cents. So if XYZ closed at 40 ½ it would open at 40. This does not mean that the stock has to actually open at 40, the stock may open at 41, but if it did open at 41, it would show on the quote screen as being up 1 point as opposed to being up ½ point (remember it closed the night before at 40 ½).

So if you had a good until cancelled order in to buy 100 shares at 40, they would adjust your order down by ½ point to read "Buy 100 XYZ at 39 ½ GTC".

To avoid your order being reduced on ex-dividend day, simply tell your broker to leave put your GTC order in as a "Do not reduce" order. This means they will not reduce your order by the amount of the dividend on ex-dividend day.

CHAPTER SIX

SPREADS

A spread is simply owning one option on a company and selling another option of the same company but either a different strike price or different month.

BULL SPREAD

Let's say that Mr. Jones is long 10 calls in Microsoft October 50 calls. Microsoft is selling at 53 and his chart work tells him it will move to 58 where the next resistance level is. He put all his discretionary funds into the options when he bought them at 5. He feels very confident that Microsoft is going to move up to 55 before his options expire in two months.

But suddenly an emergency arises and Mr. Jones has to come up with $2000. He doesn't wish to sell any of the stocks in his portfolio and he doesn't want to sell the Microsoft October 50 calls that he owns. But he looks in the paper and sees that there is a Microsoft October 60 call that is selling for $2. So he sells the Microsoft October 60 call and gets $2000 (less commission) which he uses to spend on his emergency.

On option expiration day Microsoft is indeed trading at 58. Mr. Jones sells his Microsoft October 50 calls at $8 for a $3,000 profit and lets the Microsoft October 60 calls expire worthless, thus realizing another $2000 profit (which he had already spent on his emergency).

If Microsoft had run up to Mr. Jones' target of 58 before the option expiration date and Mr. Jones wanted to sell out his Microsoft October 50 calls, he would have had to buy back his short position in the Microsoft October 60 calls when he sold out his long position in the Microsoft October 50 calls. Depending on the "time premium" left in the calls, he could either realize a profit or a loss in the October 60 calls.

For example, if there was only a week left until October option expiration when Microsoft runs up to 58, then the likelihood is that the time premium left in the October 60 calls would be less than $2 since there is only a week to go and the option is 2 points "out of the money". However, if there are 6 weeks left to go then there is a likelihood that the Microsoft October 60 call would be selling for more than $2 and he would have to buy them back at a loss.

So, let's assume that there are six weeks left to go in the October calls when Microsoft moves up to 58. The October 50 calls are selling for 9 and the October 60 calls are selling at 3. Mr. Jones would sell out his October 50 calls at 9 and realize a $4000 profit (he paid 5 for the 10 calls...$400 x 10 = $4000). He would also buy back the October 60 calls for 3 and realize a $1000 loss (he sold them at $2 or $200 per call times 10 = $2000...he bought them back at $3 or $300 per call times 10 = $3000). So his net gain on the transaction (not counting the commission which we did not calculate in this example) is $3000 ($4000 profit on the October 50's less $1000 loss on the buy back of the October 60's). This is an example of a BULL SPREAD.

BEAR SPREAD

The mirror image of this is if Mr. Jones owned the October 50 PUTS thinking that Microsoft would be moving down to 42. He sells the October 40 puts against the October 50 put position and brings in $2000. If, on option expiration day Microsoft is ABOVE 40, then Mr. Jones does not have to buy back his short October 40 put position. If, however, Microsoft is BELOW 40, then Mr. Jones must buy back the short October 40 put position when he sells his long October 50 put position.

An example would be: Mr. Jones pays $5 a put for 10 puts in Microsoft October 50 puts (for a total of $5000 plus commissions) when Microsoft is trading at 48 (it is two points IN the money and has a 3 point premium above the intrinsic value). He then sells the Microsoft October 40 put at $2 for proceeds of $2000 (less commission). On October option expiration day, Microsoft is selling at $42 and Mr. Jones' LONG 50 puts are selling at 8 (intrinsic value since it is 8 points in the money). So by selling them at $8 ($8000 total proceeds less commission) he realizes a $3000. Since the October 40 puts that he is SHORT are two points out of the money, they expire and he also realizes a $2000 gain from that short position.

Let us assume that Microsoft is at $36 on option expiration day. The LONG October 50 put would be worth $14 a put or $14,000. Mr. Jones would realize a $9000 in the sale of this long position. The Microsoft 40 put would be worth $4 so his cost of buying back these 10 puts would be $4000. Since he sold them originally at $2000 he would realize a $2000 loss on this short position. So his overall profit on the trade would be $7000 ($9000 profit on the 50 puts less the $2000 loss on the 40 put). This is an example of a BEAR SPREAD. All spreads must be done in a margin account, but there is no margin requirement for a spread aside from the requirement necessary to maintain a margin account, which is $2000 (equity options do not count toward equity).

There are many reasons why a person would wish to put on a spread. Two very good reasons are to limit risk (as in the case of Mr. M in an earlier chapter) and to lower margin requirements.

As I stated in an earlier chapter, margin requirements vary from brokerage house to brokerage house. So, for simplicity sake, let us assume a straight 30% margin requirement for a short option position (in reality you would also add how much the option is in the money and subtract how much the option is out of the money when figuring margin requirements on short positions, but I do not wish to get too complicated in this example. Your broker will be able to figure out your requirements if you decide to do naked options.)

Microsoft is selling at $50 a share and you wish to short 10 Microsoft October 50 puts which are selling at $3 for a total of $3000 (less commission). In this example, the margin requirement on the short position would be $30% of $50,000 or $15,000 (in reality the cost of the option is added or subtracted in the calculations but we are going for simplicity here).

If Mr. Jones were to short ten $50 puts and BUY ten 40 puts, his requirements would be the difference in the spread (which is 10 points...50 – 40) or $10,000. So in this example the requirements would be $5000 less by putting on a spread as opposed to doing a straight naked put position.

This also limits Mr. Jones risk on the transaction in case something unforeseeable would happen and Microsoft would plummet.

CALENDAR SPREADS

A calendar spread is a spread of one month versus another month. It can be the same strike price or a different strike price.

For example: It is September and Mr. Jones is long the January 50 calls for Microsoft for which he paid $3. He is fearful that the September/October time period for the markets will be difficult for the markets and he notices that the October 50 calls are selling for $4 while his January calls are selling for $5.

He also notices that there is a small open interest of 20 and a ½ point spread between the bid and ask on the January 50 calls, so that if he sold them at the bid side, he would get $4 ½ and if he wanted to buy them back he would have to pay $5. On the other hand the October 50 calls have an open interest of 3000 and the bid and ask has only a 1/8 point spread. If he wanted to sell the October 50 calls he could get 4 and if wanted to buy them he would pay 4 1/8. So he sells the October 50 calls short against his January 50 calls creating a CALENDAR SPREAD. This must be done in a margin account but there is no margin requirement aside from the margin requirement equity of $2000 for all margin accounts.

OPTIONS AND RETIREMENT ACCOUNTS

The only option transactions permitted in an IRA account (Individual Retirement account) is covered call writing (selling calls against stock) and buying puts in a stock that you own in the IRA account.

I have only seen an exception to this rule once in 35 years. An investor had $2,000,000 in treasury bills in his IRA and wished to short naked puts for a small amount. The brokerage firm allowed this and to this day I do not know how this happened since naked puts must be short in a margin account and IRA accounts can not have margin accounts. But it happened.

SHORT STOCK, SHORT PUT

If someone buys 100 shares of General Electric and sells 1 call of General Electric, this is a "covered" write. If someone shorts 100 shares of General Electric and shorts 1 put of General Electric, this is also a covered write.

By no stretch of the imagination are the two anywhere near equal as far as investment strategy goes. Buying 100 shares of stock and selling one call is a conservative approach. Shorting 100 shares of a stock, whether one sells a put or not, is always a highly speculative transaction.

If Mr. Smith bought 100 shares of General Electric at 50 and sold the nearest month 55 call for 2 ½ and the stock went up above 55 on option expiration day, Mr. Smith would have the stock called away at 55 and would make 5 points on the stock and 2 ½ points on the option for a total of 7 ½ points.

If Mr. Jones shorted 100 shares of General Electric at 50 and sold the nearest month 45 put for 2 ½ and the stock went down below 45 on option expiration day, Mr. Jones would be put the stock at 45 and would make 5 points on the short (50 – 45 = 5) and 2 ½ points on the option for a total of 7 ½ points.

As far as the mechanics of shorting a stock and shorting a put are concerned it is a covered write, but as far as the suitability of such a transaction, it is highly speculative.

To take it a step further, if Mr. Smith bought General Electric at 50 and sold the near month 55 call at 2 ½ and at the same time wanted to protect himself against a potential melt down in the stock, so he bought the near month 45 put for 2 ½. This would protect him against any loss greater than 10% (5 points) while at the same time limiting any profit on the transaction to 10%.

If Mr. Jones shorted General Electric at 50 and shorted the 45 puts for 2 ½ and wanted to protect himself against a possible run up in the stock, he could buy the 55 call. This would have the same protection in the opposite direction as what Mr. Smith did on the long side of General Electric. Mr. Jones would assure himself a no greater loss than

10% (50 to 55) while at the same time he would

limit his potential profit to by being short the put.

CHAPTER SEVEN

PICKING A STOCK TO WRITE CALLS

AGAINST

The easy part is learning about writing call options against a stock. The hard part is picking a stock that isn't going to be the next Enron or WorldCom. All one has to do is look at Wall Street's recommendations on Enron on the way down to see that using Wall Street's analysts as your guide would not have prevented disaster in this stock (see illustration 1). You can also see that the technical signals gave a warning when the stock was in the 80's of a technical breakdown or "sell signal".

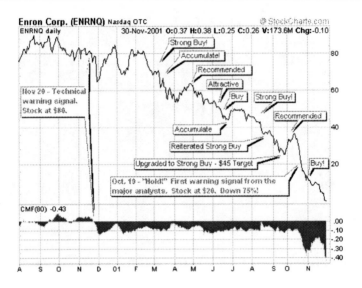

chart courtesy of stockcharts.com

ILLUSTRATION 1

Different technicians use different methods in doing their chart work. There is bar charting, point and figure charting, Elliot wave charting, Candlestick charting, just to mention a few. And within these charts there are numerous indicators: Bollinger bands, On balance volume, relative

strength, moving averages, MACD, stochastics, money flow analysis, and many more.

Some people are not so inclined toward the technical side, and I don't know why anyone would not want this in their arsenal of tools, but I have met people who do not wish to use these tools. In fact a friend of mine calls it voodoo...well, voodoo or not, if it works...If one is drawn more to the fundamental, then I would start out by finding a good money manager or mutual fund that you like and look at their top ten holdings. You can find the mutual fund top ten holdings at Yahoo's financial website. I would then look at each of the stocks in their top ten or top twenty and look at the debt...in this market environment I like to find stocks that are selling below book value and have a good cash position. The next step is to look at the premium on the options (or if in fact they even have options).

I happen to like one growth money manager that I will not mention by name, but they share their name with a common tree. This money manager did extremely well during the growth stock heyday, but during the 2000-2002 periods they have gotten clobbered like most growth money managers.

Juniper Networks is one of the stocks that I got from their portfolio. And as of this date it has been very good to me in my option writing program, as I mentioned before. I have purchased the stock below $7 ½ a share and immediately written the current month option expiration with less than 4 weeks to go in most cases and gotten $0.75 to $0.80

each time. This amounts to a 10% return on my money in a month or if I were able to do that 12 times a year, a 120% return a year.

Another good idea is to subscribe to as many financial newsletters as your budget will allow. I have gotten several good ideas from financial newsletters. Two in particular were Élan, which is an Irish pharmaceutical company and Mirant which is a company that was a break off from Southern Company. At first I was extremely afraid of Mirant because of its appearance of being similar to Enron in its description, but when August 14th came and went and there did not seem to be any shoes dropping regarding the company's balance sheet, I investigated further.

The stock was selling at \$2.95 a share and I noticed that with 4 weeks left in the September 2 ½ calls that they were selling for .80. This meant that if I bought the stock at 2.95 and sold the September 2 ½ calls at .80 that I would only have to come up with 2.15 a share for the stock and if it was called away at 2.50 I would make over 16% on my money in 4 weeks. I also noticed that Mirant had \$2.43 a share in cash with a book value of \$13.00 a share.

Both Juniper and Mirant are examples of when I ignored the technicals which did not look good at all in either of those stocks, and went with the "fundamentals". So far it has proven to be a very lucrative investment.

Elan was an example of a stock that I got from a newsletter and watched. When the chart appeared to be in a trading channel (see illustration 2.

chart courtesy of stockcharts.com

ILLUSTRATION 2

I bought the stock at 1.60 and wrote the 30 day 2 ½ calls at .25. I was looking for the 18% return that the option write gave me, not really thinking that the stock would actually be called away from me at 2.50 for a 77% return in a little over one month, but it happened.

INSIDER BUYING AND SELLING

Another statistic that is easy to find for free on the internet at yahoo financial is insider buying and selling. Not wishing to beat a dead horse by mentioning World Com and Enron over and over, but if you looked at the insider buying and selling on both of these stocks for months before their demise, you would have seen a tremendous amount of insider selling.

It is not necessarily a sign of an imminent move to the upside to see a lot of insider buying in a stock, but it can help you sleep better at night if you buy a stock and you know that one of the officers just got through buying a million shares for himself. I have also not seen any companies that have gone defunct right after someone high up in the company has bought a significant amount of shares.

If one is looking to buy a stock and write calls, then it is not necessary to have a stock go up significantly. You just don't want the stock to go down significantly.

INSTITUTIONAL HOLDINGS

Another piece of information that is readily available on the internet is the institutional holders of a company. If 50% of the outstanding shares of a company are held by institutions such as mutual funds, then it is just another plus. This statistic in and of itself however does not mean a tremendous amount as the institutional holdings in Enron and WorldCom were quite high at the end.

CHAPTER EIGHT

TECHNICAL ANALYSIS

As I mentioned in the last chapter, technical analysis involves many aspects. The person that I admire the most in the technical analysis arena is John Murphy. Anyone who is a student of technical analysis should definitely own "Technical Analysis of the Financial Markets" by John Murphy. My library of books on technical analysis is extensive but my two bibles are John Murphy's book and "Technical Analysis of Stock Trends by Edwards and McGee. The latter book was in its 16th printing in 1987 and its first edition was in 1948. When you read that book you realize that nothing changes over time. Charts are still charts no matter whether it is 1938 or 1998.

I have a simple rule of thumb when it comes to trends. I use three moving averages, the 10 day, the 50 day and the 200 day moving averages. My ideal situation is when the 10 day is above the 50 day moving average and the 50 day moving average is above the 200 day moving average. When the 10 day moving average moves below the 50 day moving average this is a warning sign to me. When the 50 day moving average crosses below the 200 day moving average (termed "the cross of death") this is a full blown exit sign for me. Of course the opposite is also true. If I am short a stock or own puts in a stock and the 50 day moving average crosses above the 200 day moving average, I use this as a sign to exit my short and go long.

If you look at the chart of the NASDAQ, in illustration 3, you will see that if you had used this as your guide, you would have saved a tremendous amount of money in this bear market (or made a tremendous amount of money if you were short).

chart courtesy of stockcharts.com

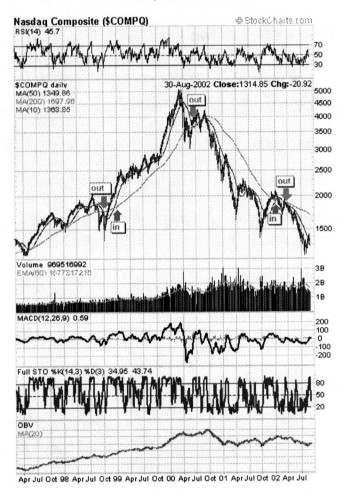

ILLUSTRATION 3

As I said before this is a very simplistic approach but it works well with trends. During a consolidation pattern, one in which a stock is going sideways, this can be a real whipsawing indicator. In the previous chart of the NASDAQ we don't really see any such pattern taking place, but it can occur, as is indicated in the chart below of Coca Cola.

I recommend finding any chart of any company and going back over any period of time, whether it is one year or ten years, and see if this technique of buying a stock when the 50 day moving average crosses above the 200 day moving average and exiting the position when the 50 day moving average crossed below the 200 day moving average. I think you will find that you would have done

Thomas H. Yarborough

extremely well following this strategy. We had been spoiled for so many years of a bull market that using this type of strategy did not seem to be important. A bear market, however, can shed much light on the necessity to have an investing discipline other than "buy and hold". There are many people suffering right now who practiced that strategy with Lucent, or Corning Glass. These are just two of many (ex) blue chip companies that have had unbelievable drops and have hurt many widows and orphans that chose to "buy and hold."

I don't want to give the impression that there has never been an instance of a stock chart looking fantastic, with the 50 day moving average above the 200 day moving average and the MACD looks strong and the On Balance Volume looks strong only to have the stock gap down 30 or 40%. This

does happen, but in my experience, it happens very

infrequently.

Chart courtesy of stockcharts.com

ILLUSTRATION 4

In illustration 4 of KO, is a good example of how the 50 day moving average can fluctuate above and below the 200 day moving average in a consolidating pattern. I tried to find a chart that would give the best example of this, but even in this chart you can see that if you had used the 50 day moving average crossover of the 200 day moving average as your entrance and exit signals, you would have been ahead of the game, albeit not by much.

To give an indication of how this strategy would have helped in a disaster situation, let's look at the chart on Enron in illustration 5.

ILLUSTRATION 5

As you can see, you would have exited Enron at

80 and would not have been back in the stock after

that time.

CHAPTER NINE

SHORTER TERM INDICATORS

For those who are shorter term oriented the 50 day moving average and the 10 day moving average can be a helpful tool. When a stock or index is trading above the 50 day moving average, a test of the moving average is a good place to be a buyer. When a stock is trading below the 50 day moving average, a test of that moving average is a good place to go short. In illustration 6 you can see how this has been helpful as a short term indicator in the QQQ over the past 2 years.

One would have used a buy stop order on the QQQ any time that the 10 day moving average crossed above the 50 day moving average.

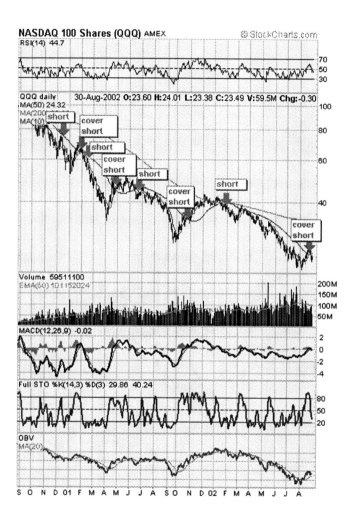

chart courtesy of stockcharts.com

ILLUSTRATION 6

WEEKLY AND MONTHLY MOVING

AVERAGES

As a follow up to looking at the 10, 50 and 200 day moving averages, I also take a look at the 10, 50 and 200 week moving averages and the 10, 50 and 200 month moving averages. It is amazing sometimes that the weekly and monthly charts will reveal an area to be cognizant of where you least suspect it.

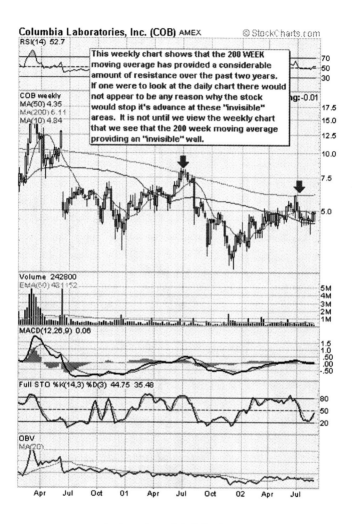

chart courtesy of stockcharts.com

ILLUSTRATION 7

Thomas H. Yarborough

chart courtesy of stockcharts.com

ILLUSTRATION 8

102

BOLLINGER BANDS

Another helpful tool in trading is the Bollinger Bands. I would highly recommend that a person use the Bollinger Bands as an investment tool. I would also recommend getting a book written by John Bollinger who is the founder of the Bollinger Bands.

Without going into too much detail, let me say that it is very helpful in determining when a stock is overbought or oversold based on the Bollinger Bands. When a stock has reached the upper end of the Bollinger Bands it is a good time to either take profits or sell short depending on what the chart pattern looks like.

If a stock is at the lower end of the band it is a good time to either cover shorts or go long depending, again on what the chart pattern looks like.

In illustration 7, the Bollinger Bands show when the stock was overbought and gave a good indication of when one might be putting on shorts and covering shorts. Again this is a good tool to use in conjunction with moving averages to determine which direction a stock or index is moving and whether one should be playing the long side or the short side.

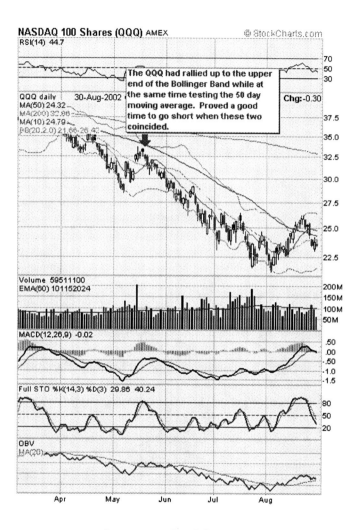

chart courtesy of stockcharts.com

ILLUSTRATION 9

You can see from the above illustration that for the most part the QQQ has had a difficult time getting above the middle band of the Bollinger Band. This is a sign of a weak market.

STOCHASTICS

Another good indicator to use when looking for the overbought or oversold nature of the market is the Stochastic. One can look at the fast stochastic, the slow stochastic and the full stochastic. Again, this is another tool in your tool chest. Just as a homebuilder needs a saw, a hammer, and a screwdriver, to build a house, so does a technician need to look at moving averages, **Bollinger Bands,** stochastics and On Balance Volume.

Illustration 8 shows when the stochastics were overbought and when they were oversold. When the stochastics were overbought proved to be a good place to look to sell. And when the stochastics were oversold it often proved to be a good place to cover shorts.

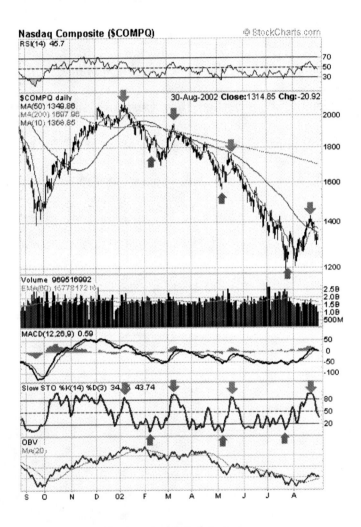

ILLUSTRATION 10

ON BALANCE VOLUME

On Balance Volume was invented by Joseph Granville in the 1960's. I remember my aunt taking the volume of each of the stocks that she owned and writing it in pencil each and every day on a long sheet of paper.

My Aunt Holly was the one who first got me interested in the stock market and technical analysis when I was 17 years of age. She leaned heavily toward following On Balance Volume in her technical work. Back then there were no computers to graph the OBV as there is now.

Basically OBV doesn't care how much a stock is up or down, it only cares about WHETHER the stock was up or down and on what volume. This is used to determine whether a stock is under accumulation or distribution. If the OBV chart is moving up, it is under accumulation, if it headed down it is under distribution.

If a stock is up a penny or up a dollar does not matter, if it is up, the volume is considered to be "buy" volume and is given a + and added to the last day's volume.

Say for example that the volume that has been added up for the previous sessions (for however long you have been charting the stock) is +1,589,300 and the stock trades 50,000 shares and is up .05 that day. The volume would now read +1,639,300. If the stock had been down .01 that day on 50,000 shares the volume would instead read +1,539,300.

The object is to then compare the volume when the stock comes back to a price that you can reference to. For example let us say that you are charting ABC Corp on 1/1/02 and you start at 0 volume and the stock is at 20 a share. The stock goes up and the stock goes down and on 4/3/02 the stock is again back to $20 a share but the volume is -385,000. The fact that there is a – in front of the volume instead of a + indicates that there has been more selling volume then buying volume and the stock is under distribution.

Again, no one has to do this anymore because of computers. Everything is in a picture.

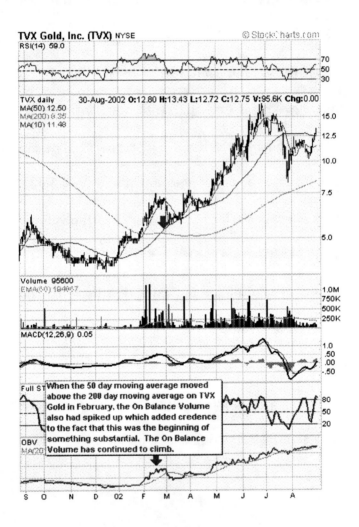

When the 50 day moving average moved above the 200 day moving average on TVX Gold in February, the On Balance Volume also had spiked up which added credence to the fact that this was the beginning of something substantial. The On Balance Volume has continued to climb.

chart courtesy of stockcharts.com

ILLUSTRATION 11

112

MOVING AVERAGE CONVERGENCE

DIVERGENCE

MACD

This indicator was developed by Gerald Appel. This combines oscillator principles with a dual moving average crossover analysis. There are two lines in this oscillator, a fast line and a slow line. The fast line, which is called the MACD line, is determined using the difference between two exponential moving averages. It is usually based on the last 12 and 26 days. The slower line is called the signal line. When the fast line crosses the slow line, it gives a signal. If it moves above the slow line it gives a buy signal and if it moves below the slow line it gives a sell signal.

The best signals are given from extreme readings. If the MACD gives a crossover sell signal from a very high level above the 0 mark it is a more valid signal than if it gives the signal closer to the 0 mark. The same is true of the buy signals, if it gives a buy signal far BELOW the 0 mark (in oversold territory) it is a more valid signal.

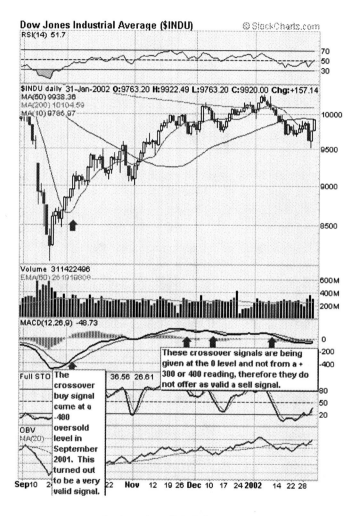

chart courtesy of stockcharts.com

ILLUSTRATION 12

SUPPORT, RESISTANCE AND TREND LINES

Technical analysis is basically a picture of human behavior, or psychology. If a person buys something and it goes down, his psychology changes from "making money" to breaking even. This area which can not be penetrated on the UPSIDE is considered <u>resistance</u>. You can think of it as a ceiling.

If a person is short a stock and it goes up, his psychology changes from "making money" to breaking even. This area which can not be penetrated on the DOWNSIDE is considered <u>support.</u> You can think of it as a floor.

When a floor is broken, it becomes a ceiling. When a ceiling is broken it becomes a floor. If you are walking along and fall through the floor, when you look up at the hole, you are looking at a ceiling.

A downtrend (or uptrend) is any three points (or more) that can be drawn on a chart to create a trend. The more times this downtrend (or uptrend) is "tested" (meaning to touch it but not penetrate it), the more viable this trend becomes.

The following illustration gives examples of support and resistance as well as a downtrend line.

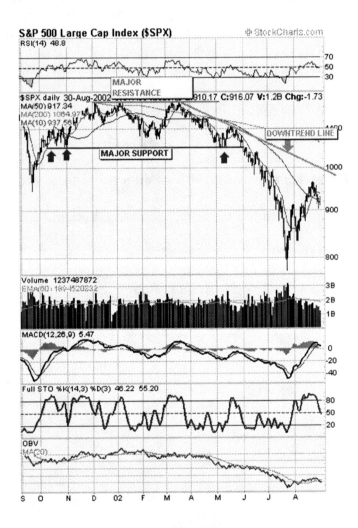

chart courtesy of stockcharts.com

ILLUSTRATION 13

POINT AND FIGURE CHARTING

Point and figure charting is an important tool in your toolbox to help determine a breakout or breakdown in a chart pattern as well as a trend.

Point and figure charting uses X's and O's as opposed to bar graphs and must have a "three point reversal" in order to change the direction of the chart.

A three point reversal on a stock above $20 a share would mean 3 one point moves from 20 to 23. On a stock below $20 a share it would mean three ½ point moves from 20 to 18 ½. With a stock below $5 a share, it would take three ¼ point moves to

change direction in the stock or to register three X's or three 0's.

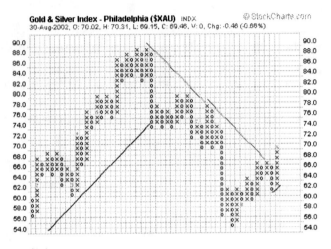

Gold & Silver Index - Philadelphia ($XAU) INDX © StockCharts.com
30-Aug-2002, O: 70.02, H: 70.31, L: 69.15, C: 69.46, V: 0, Chg: -0.46 (-0.66%)

Alert Triple Top Breakout

chart courtesy of stockcharts.com

ILLUSTRATION 14

In the last move up in the XAU notice when it hit 67 that it registered a triple top breakout. This means that it had been above 66 but had not touched 67 on two previous occasions and this had

become a formidable resistance area. By touching

67 on the third time, it registered a higher X and

broke this resistance level.

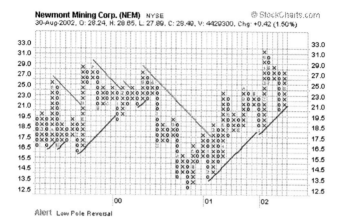

chart courtesy of stockcharts.com

ILLUSTRATION 15

Notice in the chart on Newmont Mining, that

when the chart is below $20 a share, it changes to ½

point increments.

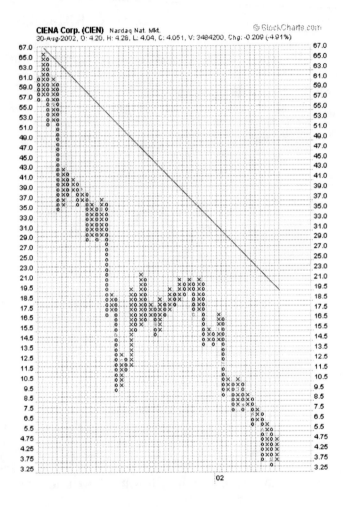

chart courtesy of stockcharts.com

ILLUSTRATION 16

As with this chart of Ciena Corporation when the stock is below $5, the chart changes from ½ point increments to ¼ point increments.

ACCUMULATION/DISTRIBUTION LINE

The Accumulation/Distribution line and the On Balance Volume line will look very similar in many cases. I prefer to look at the monthly chart on both the On Balance Volume and the Accumulation/Distribution line. As you can see from the illustration below, a turn in a stock with a validation by the Accumulation/Distribution Line gives credence to the move.

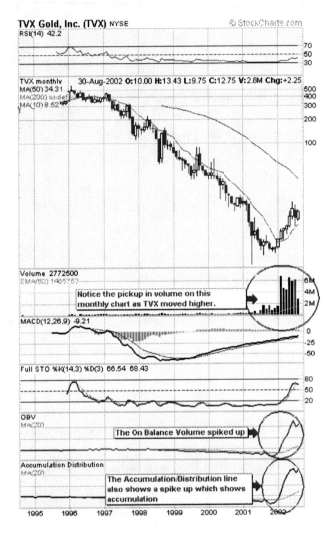

chart courtesy of stockcharts.com

ILLUSTRATION 17

COMMON TOPPING AND BOTTOMING
CHART PATTERNS

Here are some common chart patterns that are basic and common bottoming and topping patterns:

DOUBLE TOP

A double top is exactly as the name describes. It is a pattern where a price hits a high, sells off and rallies back up to that high again without penetrating it. The high in the NASDAQ in March 2000 was made with a double top formation.

chart courtesy of stockcharts.com

ILLUSTRATION 18

DOUBLE BOTTOM

A double bottom is the opposite of a double top. When prices are falling and make a low to form a support level, then rally and come back to test that support area and hold, it is a double bottom. Double bottoms and double tops can best be viewed when applying other tools in conjunction with them.

Thomas H. Yarborough

chart courtesy of stockcharts.com

ILLUSTRATION 19

128

HEAD AND SHOULDER

Another reversal formation is the "head and shoulders" and "reverse head and shoulders" formation. Just as the double bottom is the reverse of a double top, so is the reverse head and shoulders formation the reverse of the head and shoulders formation.

The head and shoulders formation is a "topping" formation and the reverse head and shoulders formation is a "bottoming" formation. It is only when the bottom of the left and right shoulder (neckline) is broken that the formation has concluded it's topping (or bottoming) process and the reverse trend starts.

There can be multiple shoulders in a head and shoulders and reverse head and shoulders formation but in the illustration below of the S+P 500 monthly chart one can clearly see a head and shoulders formation with a defined left shoulder, head and right shoulder.

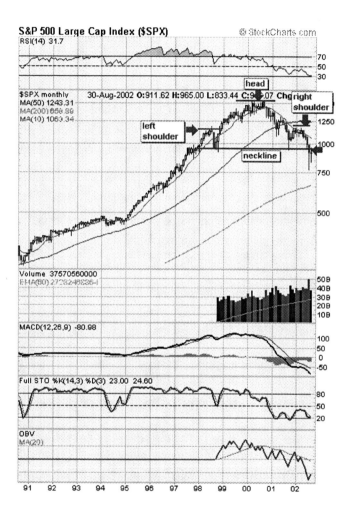

chart courtesy of stockcharts.com

ILLUSTRATION 20

Thomas H. Yarborough

FIBONACCI NUMBERS

Fibonacci numbers are a number sequence which is constructed by adding the first two numbers to arrive at the third (i.e. 1+2=3) this sequence of number is (1, 2, 3, 5, 8, 13, 21, 34, 55, 89, 144). This ratio (any number of the two to the third) is 62%. The complement of 62% is 38% (100% - 62% = 38%). Both 62% and 38% are popular Fibonacci retracement numbers.

There are now computer programs that will calculate the Fibonacci retracement levels so that calculating them by hand is no longer necessary. Below is an illustration of a chart with Fibonacci retracement lines added.

*The Basic Guide to Understanding Options
and Technical Analysis and Strategies for Their Use*

As with any of the other tools noted in this book, Fibonacci numbers are yet another tool to be used. I like to use the Fibonacci numbers in conjunction with moving averages and trend lines.

In the case of the S+P 500 chart below, the 38.2% retracement level also happens to fall at the 200 month moving average at 662. For this reason and because an interpretation of the Elliot Wave chart indicates that the S+P 500 is in a fourth wave down of a five wave decline I would use 662 as my goal on the S+P 500.

133

2

Thomas H. Yarborough

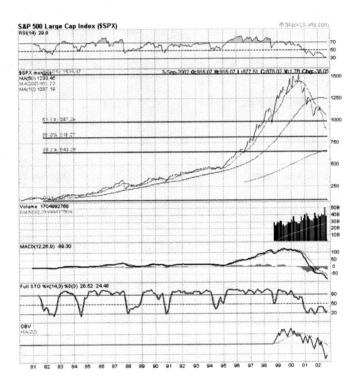

chart courtesy of stockcharts.com

ILLUSTRATION 21

VIX

The VIX is an option volatility index.

You can actually think of it as a "fear" index. I used the VIX to pick a temporary bottom on the market in the week immediately following the World Trade Center terrorist attack on 9/11/2001.

As I have said previously in this book, each of these indicators should be used in conjunction with other indicators. The more indicators you know the better a technician you become. One reason I admire John Murphy so much is because the man uses every source of technical analysis at his disposal. He will talk about the Elliott wave count of a market index (or a stock) and then talk about the VIX. He will discuss a stock testing its 50 day moving average and then point out a MACD buy signal. He uses it all and this is what makes him, in my opinion, an excellent technician.

I use the VIX mostly to determine a short term or long term market bottom. When the VIX gets to a reading above 50, I will get into the market. This usually means that the fear is so high in the market place that we are seeing a market bottom. It does not mean it is THE market bottom, but A market bottom.

As was the case on September 11, 2001, there was A market bottom and a rally ensued that lasted for several months before starting another leg (move) down.

The first chart below is a chart of the VIX from 1995 when it originated to 2002. As you can see there have been only four times that the VIX has had a reading above 50 in those seven years: October 27, 1997; October 2, 1998; September 19, 2001; and July 23, 2002.

The second chart is a chart of the S+P 500 for the corresponding period of time 1995 to 2002. I have circled the times where the VIX had a reading above 50 and as you can see, each of those times was A bottom. The rallies that resulted from those points were a minimum of 23% to a maximum of 56%.

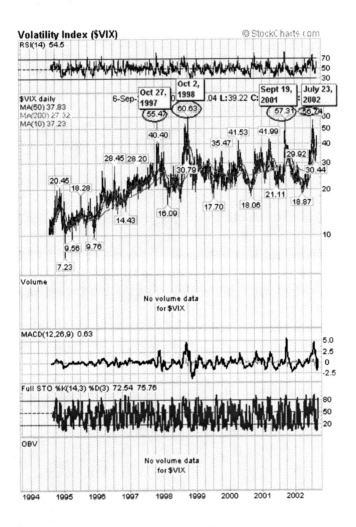

chart courtesy of stockcharts.com

ILLUSTRATION 22

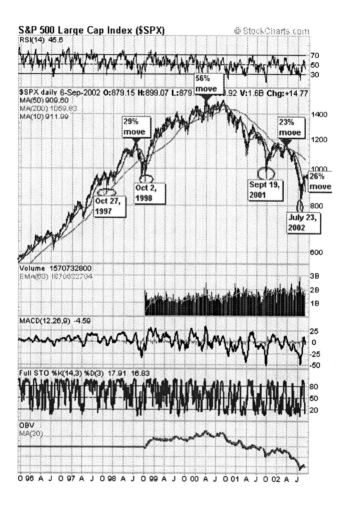

chart courtesy of stockcharts.com

ILLUSTRATION 23

CHAPTER TEN

THE WASH RULE

The "Wash Rule" simply put means that you can not sell a stock for a loss and buy it back in less than 32 days and still claim the loss on your taxes.

The IRS allows you, as of this writing, to deduct up to $3,000 a year in stock market losses against your ordinary income so many people will sell the stocks that they have a loss in at the end of the year to take advantage of that loss. They will then turn around and buy the stock back after they have "locked in" the loss.

The IRS says that is all fine and dandy as long as you don't buy the stock back in less than 32 days. So if you bought 1000 shares of Cisco at $40 a share on January 1ˢᵗ and sell it on December 31ˢᵗ at $15.00 a share, you have a $25,000 loss all of which you can offset against any gains that you have for the year in other transactions and whatever is left over you can take $3,000 of it against ordinary income.

If you had other gains of $20,000 in other stocks for the year and you took the $25,000 loss in Cisco, you would end up with a net $5,000 loss for the year of which you could reduce your income for tax purposes by $3,000 and the remaining $2,000 loss you could carry forward to the next year to offset against any gains or if you do not have any gains, to offset against your income for that year.

If, however, after selling Cisco at $15 a share on December 31ˢᵗ, you were to turn around and buy the stock again on January 29ᵗʰ (it doesn't matter what price you buy it back) of the next year, you would not be allowed to claim the loss.

The IRS wants you to be "at risk" for 32 days (actually it is 31 days but I always throw in an extra day just to be extra safe). What if Cisco is at $25 a share by the time you want to buy it back? That is exactly what the IRS wants you to think about before you sell and take the loss.

"Well, that is no problem", you think to yourself, "I will simply buy a call option on the stock". Nope. The IRS will not allow you to do that either, nor a warrant, nor a convertible bond or convertible preferred stock. They have you.

Or do they?

There is one thing you can do that is perfectly legal and limits the risk that you face by selling a stock you don't want to be out of for 30 days. You can sell an in the money put naked.

Let's take the Cisco example. You sold 1000 shares of Cisco at $15 a share on December 31st but you are afraid that Cisco will run up in price in the next 30 days before you can legally buy it back. But you see that the Cisco $25 put going out six months is selling at $12. It has an intrinsic value of $10 and a time premium of $2. If you sell the puts naked, and the stock does run up to $25, the put will be selling with no intrinsic value and all time premium.

What I would do to determine what the time premium might be in that put if it had no intrinsic value is to look at the same month put for the $15 strike price when the stock is selling at $15. If, for example, you see that the $15 put is selling at $4, you can make a guesstimate that if Cisco goes to $25 a share the put that you sold for $12 will be selling around $4 (this is not a rule set in concrete, only a guideline).

So in this case if you sold Cisco at $15 realizing a $25,000 loss and immediately sold the $25 put for $12 and 31 days later the stock is selling at $25 and the put is priced at $4, you would have paid $10,000 more for the 1000 shares of Cisco that you bought back but you would realize a profit of $8,000 in the naked put that you sold at $12 and bought back at $4, thereby only "missing out" on a 2 point move in the stock instead of a ten point move in the stock.

Of course, this would not work in an individual retirement account, but then again you can't claim any losses in your IRA anyway.

EXCERPTS

Based on the technical signals that I discussed in this book, the QQQ generated many buy and sell signals (many more sell signals then buy signals) in the past few years.

The first chart has color coded arrows which have corresponding text that indicates the signals that were given and why.

Entered NASDAQ market when 50 day moving average moved above the 200 day moving average. This is a bullish signal.

1.triple top breakout...aggressive traders add to long positions.

2-after failing to make a higher high the 50 day moving average was broken on a closing basis. Look to re-enter long position at a test of the 200 day moving average.

3-went long on a test of the 200 day moving average.

4-sold on close below 200 day moving average.

5-the 50 day moving average moved below the 200 day moving average know as the "Cross of Death" but the NASDAQ actually was trading above the 200 day moving average which made it prudent to stand aside until the picture became clearer. After the NASDAQ dropped below the 200 day moving average and rallied back up again was a time to go short.

6-NASDAQ close above the 200 day moving average. Covered short, but the 50 day moving average is still below the 200 day moving average so it is not safe to go long.

7-the NASDAQ broke below the 200 day moving average and the 10 day and 50 day moving average are both below the 200 day moving average. Go short.

8-testing low. Cover short.

9-failed to make new high and at the same time it is testing the 50 day moving average. Go short.

10-testing low again. Cover short position.

11-after breaking support, it rallied up to resistance and tested the 50 day moving average. Go short.

12-broken above the 50 day moving average. Cover shorts and look for possible rally to 200 day moving average to go short again.

12-broke below the 50 day moving average and the 10 day moving average has crossed below the 50 day moving average as well. Go short.

13-testing lows. Cover short.

14-broke support then rallied to resistance. Go short.

15-broke above the 50 day moving average. Cover short.

16-broke below the 50 day moving average and 10 day moving average has moved below the 50 day moving average. Go short.

17-18-after September 11th WTC disaster, the NASDAQ gapped below what could have been a double bottom, the VIX index (volatility index) got to an extremely high reading of 58. This has only happened two other times in the past 5 years, October 1997 and October 1998 which were panic selling bottoms in the market. Cover short positions and go long with a target of the 50 day moving average and possibly the 200 day moving average to exit long positions.

19-sell 1/2 long position. Testing the 50 day moving average. arrow/Red arrow-Testing 200 day moving average.

20-sell 2nd half of long position and go short.

21-closed above 200 day moving average. Also the 10 day moving average has crossed above the 200 day moving average. Cover shorts.

22-50 day moving average crossed above the 200 day moving average. Bullish sign. Go long.

23-broke below the 200 day moving average. Sell 1/2 long position.

24-50 day moving average crossed below the 200 day moving average. "Cross of death" Sell 2nd 1/2 of long position.

25-rallied up above 200 day moving average but the 50 day moving average was just below the 200 day moving average which made going long a difficult scenario. Stood aside to wait for additional data. The NASDAQ then broke below the 200 day moving average and rallied back up to the 200 day moving average creating a shorting opportunity.

26-tested the short term bottom. Cover short.

27-after breaking support, the NASDAQ rallied up to the 50

day moving average. Go short.

28-testing the low, cover short.

TRANSLATING THIS INTO ACTUAL TRADES

ON THE QQQ

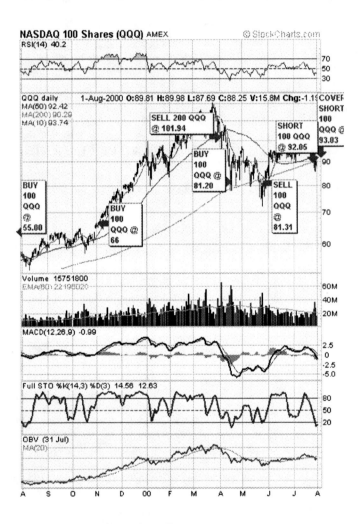

chart courtesy of stockcharts.com

The chart above depicts the actual trades that
would have taken place base on the signals
generated. This is for the period of August 1999 to
August 2000.

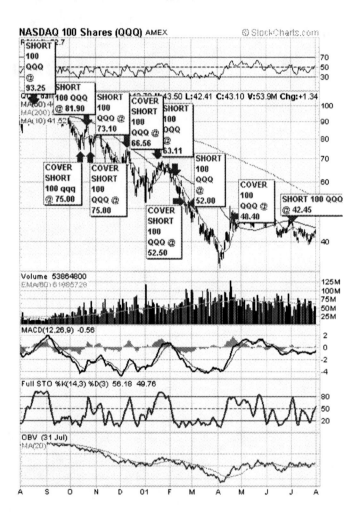

From the period of August 2000 to August 2001

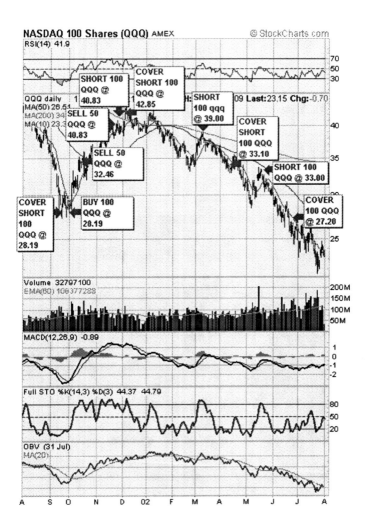

NASDAQ 100 Shares (QQQ) AMEX   © StockCharts.com

RSI(14) 41.9

COVER
SHORT
100 QQQ @
42.85

SHORT 100
QQQ @
40.83

SHORT
100 qqq
@ 39.00

COVER
SHORT
100 QQQ
@ 33.10

QQQ daily
MA(50) 26.51
MA(200) 34
MA(10) 23.3

SELL 50
QQQ @
40.83

09 Last: 23.15 Chg: -0.70

SELL 50
QQQ @
32.46

SHORT 100
QQQ @ 33.00

COVER
SHORT
100
QQQ @
28.19

BUY 100
QQQ @
28.19

COVER
100 QQQ
@ 27.20

Volume 32797100
EMA(50) 106377288

MACD(12,26,9) -0.89

Full STO %K(14,3) %D(3) 44.37 44.79

OBV (31 Jul)
MA(20)

A   S   O   N   D   02   F   M   A   M   J   J   A

From the period of August 2001 to August 2002

SOMETHING ELSE TO CONSIDER...

As I mentioned in an earlier chapter, I follow growth money managers and growth mutual funds when I pick the stocks I wish to write calls against. Some of these growth stocks are selling at $5 and below, as of the writing of this book, from their lofty prices above $100 a share. Because of this, I sometimes end up doing buy/writes (buying stock and selling calls) on some sizeable positions where the return is 10-16% in a month.

When option expiration arrives and you are faced with the decision to either buy back the call and roll it out (sell the next month call) or allow the stock to be called away from you, here is something to consider: Let us assume that PMC Sierra is at $5.15 a share and the expiring $5.00 calls are quoted 0.15 bid to 0.20 offered. Since these options will trade in nickel increments (.05, .10, .15, .20, etc.) but the stock will trade in penny increments (5.14, 5.15, 5.16, 5.17, etc.) it behooves you to take this into consideration.

Are you better off buying back the expiring option at the offer side of .20 or are you better off letting the stock be called away at $5.00 and then putting the trade on again? I have always opted to let the stock be called away. The reason is because if you are buying 20,000 shares of stock and writing 200 calls, then each penny amounts to $200, so a nickel equals $1,000.

The other thing to consider is your transaction costs. In many cases you can get a trade on a stock done (especially a NASDAQ stock) at $50.00, however with options, the clearing costs are from $1.00 an option to $1.50 an option, so if you bought back the 200 calls at $.20, you would be paying $4,000 plus at least $200 in commissions, whereas if you just let the stock be called away your transaction costs would more than likely be much less than that.

I look at the chart on the stock in many cases to see if the stock is on support or resistance when option expiration day rolls around and this also influences my decision. For example, if a stock has just run up from $5.00 to $7.70 and resistance is at $8.00 where the 50 day moving average is, then I will allow the stock to be called away and wait for the stock to pull back (assuming I have the $7.50 calls written).

If, however, a stock has just pulled back from $8.00 or so to $5.15 and the chart shows that there is good solid support between $5.00 and $5.25 a share, I may not risk being out of the stock and may opt to buy back the $5 call and roll out to the next month. So, even if the expiring option is quoted $0.15 to 0.20 and the next month option is trading at $0.70 to 0.75, I will put a "spread" order in to buy back the current month and sell the next month at a "$0.50 credit". This means that if they buy back the current month at $0.20 (or the offer side) and sell the next month at $0.70 (or the bid side) I will end up with a $0.50 credit per call. This works out to be better than a 10% return on my $5.00 a share stock so rather than risk the numbers changing overnight by having the stock run, I will just roll the option out.

If on the other hand the spread is too high between the bid and ask on either of these options, then I will wait, allowing the stock to be called away.

For example, if the current month was quoted $0.15 to 0.25 or the next month was quoted $0.65 to $0.75 I may still put the order in as a spread order (selling it for a $0.50 credit) hoping that the trading desk can get the order filled in the middle, but if it doesn't get filled I will just let the stock be called away.

QUIZ

1) On April 10th you buy 10 calls of KO January 45 calls (expiring this coming January) for a price of 6 ½ when the stock is trading at 49 ½. On January 21st when the calls are due to expire, KO is trading at 53 ½. Based on this information answers the following questions.

How much time premium did you pay for the calls when you purchased them?

On January 21st what should be the price of the option?

How much did you make?

What was your return?

2) On April `10th you buy 1000 shares of Intel at 14 ½ and sell the July 15 calls for 1 ½. Based on this information answer the following questions.

If on July option expiration day Intel is selling at $18. What will be the result and what will be your total return.

If on July option expiration day Intel is selling at 14.90. What will be the result and what will be your total return.

3) On April 10th you do a bear spread on Microsoft, selling 10 July 50 calls and buying 10 July 55 calls for a two point credit spread while Microsoft is selling at 49 ½. Based on this information answer the following questions:

What is your margin requirement on this position?

On July option expiration Microsoft is selling at 50 ¾. What will be required of you on this transaction to close out this position and what will be your profit or loss on this transaction based on intrinsic value?

On July option expiration Microsoft is selling at 48 ½. What will be required of you on this transaction to close out this position and what will be your profit or loss on this transaction based on intrinsic value?

4) You purchase 1000 shares of Microsoft at 50 on April 10th and buy 10 Microsoft July 45 puts at 1 ½ and sell 10 Microsoft July 55 calls at 1 ½. Based on this information answer the following questions:

On July option expiration Microsoft is selling at $35 a share. What will be your profit or loss on the transaction?

On July option expiration Microsoft is selling at $62 a share. What will be your profit or loss on the transaction?

5) On December 31st you sell out your 200 shares of JDS Uniphase that you paid $140.00 a share for on July 10th. You sell the 200 shares at $3.00 a share. You had a short term capital gains of $19,000 before the sale of JDS Uniphase.

What will be your gain or loss for tax purposes. If there is a loss, how much will be forwarded to the next year?

6) Draw a trend line on this chart.

chart courtesy of stockcharts.com

7) Draw a trend line on this chart.

chart courtesy of stockcharts.com

8) Draw two major areas of support on this chart.

Thomas H. Yarborough

chart courtesy of stockcharts.com

9) Draw a resistance line on this chart.

168

Thomas H. Yarborough

10) In this point and figure chart, if the stock trades at 57 this will be a _____?

chart courtesy of stockcharts.com

*The Basic Guide to Understanding Options
and Technical Analysis and Strategies for Their Use*

ANSWER PAGE

1)

You paid $6 ½ for the Jan 45 calls. The intrinsic value was $ 4 ½ ($49 ½ - 45 = 4 ½). Therefore you paid 2 points (time) premium (6 ½ - 4 ½ = 2).

The intrinsic value of the option is 8 ½ (53 ½ - 45 = 8 ½)

You paid 6 ½ and sold at 8 ½ therefore you made 2 points profit.

2 divided by 6 ½ = 30.8%

2)

The stock will be called at $15 a share. You paid $13,000 ($14 ½ less the 1 ½ point brought in by the sale of the calls). You realized a $2000 gain ($15,000 - $13,000 = $2,000) or a 15.38% return ($2,000 divided by $13,000).

The option will expire worthless. You will have realized a $1500 gain on the call or 11 ½ % on your money invested ($13,000) and you are free to write another call against your stock position.

3)

$5,000. Each spread is 5 points and there are 10 calls. Each call represents 100 shares of stock, therefore 5 x 10 = 50. 50 x 100 = 5,000.

Buy back the 10 $50 calls at intrinsic value which is ¾ for a cost of $750.

You received a $2,000 credit on the spread when you wrote them, therefore your profit would be $2,000 - $750 = $1250. The $55 calls will expire worthless since they are out of the money.

All options expire worthless therefore the $2,000 credit which you received when you wrote the calls is your profit.

4)

$5,000. You exercise the $45 put therefore your loss is your cost of $50 a share x 1000 = $50,000 less your sale (put) at $45 a share = $45,000 for a total loss of $5,000

Stock is called at $55 a share x 1000 shares = $55,000. Your cost was $50 a share x 1000 = $50,000 therefore you have a $5,000 gain.

5) $28,000 - $600 = $27,400 less $19,000 in gains = $8,400.

$3,000 can be taken against ordinary income and $5,400 loss will be carry forwarded to the next year.

6)

chart courtesy of stockcharts.com

7)

Thomas H. Yarborough

chart courtesy of stockcharts.com

8)

chart courtesy of stockcharts.com

9)

chart courtesy of stockcharts.com

10) Double Top Breakout.

More information can be found on the strategies mentioned in this book

at www.bullbearstragies.com

Thomas H. Yarborough

TESTIMONIALS

Tom's experience and expertise in the market in conjunction with his knowledge of technical analysis has been invaluable to me as an institutional trader. Furthermore, although I was initially dubious about technical analysis, he has consistently called the market correctly.

Benedikt Palmason

Investment Manager, London, England

Today's marketplace is very hard to keep up with. The way the markets have been for the last few years has been unprecedented and regular methods have sometimes been useless when trying to read into market movements. Swift changes have rattled the market and it is at times like this that one thing is more valuable than other - experience. Tom has time and again showed me that by combining experience, general knowledge about the market along with very good options and technical analysis expertise you can get the winning formula. His knowledge in various fields has put him in a place where I can only hope to be one day. On many occasions he has hinted me on things I would never had seen through the jungle of information I read every day. And in modern day markets it is invaluable.

To name one good example of many, he emailed me on September 10th 2001 predicting that the S+P 500, which had closed that day at 1080 was on support but that he expected it to break that support area and have a capitulation sell off on some news event. The following day, set up for the capitulation sell off that occurred when the market reopened on September 17th. He then sent me an email telling us to buy the market as the VIX had gotten over 50 and the panic selling so great that this was the capitulation sell off that he had been looking to buy into. I have come to rely on his expertise in my decision making process as an institutional trader and I give him my very best recommendations...

Thomas H. Yarborough

Mr. T. Johannsson

Institutional Trader, Reykjavik, Iceland

I met Tom a year ago on his visit to Luxembourg. Since then, we've been exchanging our views on the stock market. He has been of very precious help in confirming fundamental trends and relying on a precise technical analysis. His knowledge of options is one of his numerous strengths and thanks to this we could elaborate some interesting strategies. Always available when you need him, he answers your questions in minimum delays and with accuracy. Nowadays, he's my favorite person to talk to as a strategic and wise advisor on stock markets.

Catherine

Institutional Trader

Luxembourg

I have been using Tom's charts for some time now and his technical expertise and insight of the market conditions have given me some ideas on how to manage my trades. He has through his experience managed to spot an opportunity when there is one. He has also recommended certain strategies to protect positions.

Birnir Institutional Trader

Reykjavik Iceland

Thomas H. Yarborough

ABOUT THE AUTHOR

Thomas Yarborough started to learn about technical analysis from his aunt in 1965 even before going to Guilford College to major in economics. He started working in the brokerage business in 1970 and by the time that he left UBSPaineWebber in 2001 he was a million dollar producer specializing in foreign institutional business, sharing his technical analysis and option strategies with traders who came to rely on his input.

Printed in the United States
78663LV00001B/71